THE PLUTO SUMMER

An Intergalactic Romantic Date

ROBERT DAWSON

Copyright © 2021 by Robert Dawson

All rights reserved. No part of this publication may be reproduced, distributed, or transmitted in any form or by any means, including photocopying, recording, or other electronic or mechanical methods, without the prior written permission of the publisher, except in the case of brief quotations embodied in critical reviews and certain other noncommercial uses permitted by copyright law.

Book Design by Aeyshaa

Elevation at 600

We're up there, ears popping

Heart racing through the hills

Don't look down if you're scared

Down your spine, sudden chills

Any time spent with you

It is well worth it

There is beauty in the danger

Sharing air space with strangers

Citizens from other worlds

Nod their heads as we roam skies

Honing in on this great surprise

I've got something to show you

315

I've seen worlds spark my desires

Tasted candy from overseas

Sparked leaves in California

Watched her dance by the beach

Lied and been ungodly

Eyes rolled when the wise tried to counsel

Drawing closer to the above and underneath

Is it really love that grants peace?

When I'm sleeping, do I leave my body?

What if you're all I've dreamt of?

It's fascinating to ponder

I'm fond of you and all your beauty

My fingers wave through dimensions

Flirting with worlds unseen

Worthy of you in this lifetime

Take my hand; I deserve it

You deserve it too

After Three Puffs

Earth is ugly and drenched in sin

Liars lead the way

Sluts own the evening

Vodka with a chase

Lipstick on collars

Long strokes after two

Last names don't matter

The bar doesn't ask for age

No era, new age, nothing feels the same

We covet the game

Set traps, no longer chases

Sit and take it

Fabricated and long-winded

Earth benders move the waters

Fire spitters live in Vegas

Surgery makes them ageless

When shall we move to Pluto?

White man wants to head to mars

This is getting ugly No one is getting that far

Air, land, and Sea

I love you with my mind

Air, land, and sea

Dancing slowly

Capturing time as you move

What did I do to deserve this?

An average sinner who knows the truth

Utter things with no rebuke

Vulgar in approach, it's okay to be loose

Lifted through the buds, watching waters move

Be grateful always

Fight for the right to choose and for heaven's sake

Choose wisely

Talking

Talk to me. I got time

Bright ideas on dark skies

I love your Afro

That lovely dark brown hue

Smile, that gap looks perfect on you

What do you say we take a trip?

Let's dive deep in

Love, I can sink my teeth in

Reality, I can hold

In a world full of lies

I'm your truth

While today is still today

The seatbelts keep us safe

With each journey, there's a risk

I stare at you, and I'm convinced

I found forever in mortal form

All

Locked in

Blot out any doubt

I'm all you require

You're all I could ever desire

Should we lift off

Fly far away from here

Soaring until all we know disappears

I've got a lifetime for you

By the water, it's beautiful

Air land and sea

I've welcomed the idea in my heart

Left past where it belongs

Dark matter thoughts

Earth

Where the blue live for the green

Men say hello to dive in-between

In and out of time with screens

In and out of sight, we scream

We dream and don't deliver

We live to remember

But dismember

Each other over oil and space

Do we need to expand?

Past this fragile blue place

What agenda should we chase?

I needed you to hear me beyond

What you consider faith

Instead is what I dread

We both desired space

I headed to mars

Not knowing what I was

In search of

The Pluto summer

A love I only heard of

Just believing it exists

You and I are a risk

Only I leap like this

A secret you can't keep like this

No matter the destruction

Under the influence

Dramatically changing our production

This world may not be here

For our kinds reproduction

Is the future up for discussion

Is reality where it is for us

Departing Pluto

Love is for me. Yes it is

We know exactly who we are

Sunsets on the beach

My ego's beneath me

Maturity grounds you in the end

I hear voices harmonizing with the wind

I'm captivated by your gap and lovely brown skin

You feel like the perfect love song

I just wanna play you on repeat

You are my favorite love song

Singing you while in the streets

I feel so good; it's okay to feel good

We should get in our feelings for a while

I feel special on a cellular level

To go without a phone for days

The immense joy

With all I need

The vows I give to have and hold on too

When fires rage in hostile environments

Foreign aircraft roam the skies

I'm here still holding

Still loving as we journey

Earth tones

Brown was here first

You light a fire in my pants

Look at your hue

Earth tone lips don't tease me

I desire you before breakfast

Tell me you like that necklace

Thank you for curing my reckless

Holding me captive with a kiss

Black sand beaches and red wine

You can't handle the smoke, but you try

I want you for a lifetime

Just know I'll try

Held tightly in my heart

We both know why

I'm a forever kind of guy

You're a special type of fly

So I embrace this journey with you

You light a fire in my pants

The Pluto summer

I'm thinking you should put it out

This bottle is almost empty

The moon is getting tired

The way it shines on your skin

All the ways your spine can bend

We need more hours

Can we borrow from tomorrow?

I'm playing in your Afro

While you're pulling on my dreads

You can haunt my every nightmare

As long as I put you to bed

Eye contact

Drawing closer to forever

Her hands, they heal

She runs them through my dreads

At the climax of my emotions

She cums inside my head

Nobody, and I mean, nobody

That has ever received breath

in a human form is like her

We kiss under a distant moon

Staring up to a foreign sky, green clouds

Tell me how you love my body

Stroke my dreads in the evening

I give you flowers while your heart is beating

You give me those forever vibes

Hundreds of ancient tribes sacrificed and thrived

I live in the present with you in mind

Heading to Pluto

I hear fearful high notes in my ears

Sopranos in full force

I'm trippin'

Up, up and away

I'm drifting far beyond the clouds

You can come with me

Just be too loud out here

I've seen things you can't explain

Forgot worlds I should have retained

I realized I wasn't getting younger

Brainstorm through hail and thunder

To create a much better version of self

You, my dear, are added wealth

Please don't adhere to the risk

This is a gift worth giving, I'm certain

Because of death, each breath is worth living

Chances to advance us are made without fear

You'll only shake for a lil bit

Robert Dawson

Then gravity takes over

Just accept it and feel fine

We'll be there in no time

Her color

Her color is real brown like earth in the beginning

When the sun hits, she shines

Oh Lord, what a sight

You should see her at night

The moon sneaks a glare

My thirst increases

We sit by water take pictures without filters

Vibrant touches kisses that carry weight

Honest

The high and lows

Thoughts in between

Actions that go unseen

Lies told in hopes to be free

Impossible

Only the truth bare and naked

Sets you free

Earth life ain't free

Knowledge ain't cheap

At times a burden

Lays with you while you sleep

Slowly drowning you to denial

Who can stand up?

To themselves in truth

Not many

We found love in Mississippi

Robert Dawson

I found out I was in love In Mississippi

We were separate by thousands of miles

She kept lingering

In my subconscious

I've never missed like this

Indeed my heart grew fonder

Pondering on the future

Kisses and tribal dances

The crowd cheers for the honest

I await our embrace

I love her

I love her hair

It's the texture and the hue

Her gap is beautiful

Made in West Africa

She came here for me

My heart skips the beat

Played in my head

Sunsets on the beach

Watching the planes pass

Adoring the moments we share

The very fact that we're together

Makes this life seem fair

Hip thrusting in the air

The journey was harsh

I overcame slow dance to victory

We made it

Her Beautiful Dark Skin

Robert Dawson

I love her dark skin

You couldn't fathom

How much it means and what it does

How it feels when I get close

Not everything is perfect

Beauty isn't surface

I tread gently over your stretch marks

I kiss your shoulder on the beach

We found love while the world was in retreat

Forced to fear but not all believed

I stared at the Mirror and Felt Fine

The world searches for perfection

I've had that idea

Seen pain fill the valleys

Even I have shed some tears

My journey far from easy

Been moving forward for years

I'm okay with what I see

It's cool I've gotten over heartaches

Fought battles worth winning

Grinned when trouble fired shots at me

I'm so determined to watch me float

To ascend above it all

I have the highest hopes

I'm so okay here

I'm All in Now

Robert Dawson

I'm always in the mood for you

Daydreams and quiet whispers

Deliver messages from the future

I see wonders in your fro

The depth of your ideals

The very fabric of your intellect

Worn like a shirt in my subconscious

complete me

I'm completely in love. Be careful now

This means something

With my eyes closed, I've seen something

Hop in, my love

We're headed somewhere

You've never seen the moon this close up

Taken

Slim fine from New Orleans

Or thick shawty from Houston

Don't matter now; I'm taken

If I had time before, I don't now

To be loved like this, they desire

Lord knows how people envy

While the world scatters to find it

Flaunting all they have

Basking in ideas the evening life brings

I don't have to wander

She makes my aging heart sing

Up There

Bright colors on a morning sky

Earth can't be that bad

Sometimes I get weary

Then my mind drifts to you

Separated by the sea

Soon I'll shift to you

There was a vacancy

A yearning for a spark

I've got a smile

Don't you know you're the biggest part?

I feel like sprinting with reindeers

Or searching for a hollow earth

The energy of what we have

Makes everything work

There's something so special

I yield to this feeling

Gravity, please don't let me down

Does Anyone Ever Shut Up?

In all honesty, does anyone ever shut up?

Seriously all you do is sin

However, I'm not that righteous

Does anything good excite us?

With full conviction having no priors

I know no place like earth

I can't hear anything

The ugly things on screen and in hand

Disrupts the present

No idea of true perspective

Plummeting down to never make projections

This is the world of unbelief

I can't hear straight. No one ever stops talking

In Touch

My fingers roam lovely dark skin

With the brightest of ideas

Drums beat in my subconscious

My heart hurdles over lines

All because you gave me your time

I'm locked in on all your attention

My head nods right, shifting into dimensions

Where I can see you different

Just to experience a paradigm shift

No matter what it is you do it

Everything here is congruent

Yikes, love is scary

You don't have to be

At all

My eyes wander past the gorgeous tightness of your fro

With the brightest of ideas

Sweet voices invade my daydreams

We share the same religion

In Trenched

It's better we journey together

Eagles swoop down for their prey

I've listened to lies covered in sugar

That torment others during the day

Bullets move history

Not the shooters. No one remembers them

People walk past the homeless

Honing in on the fragile

The screens capture the wild

This world is cold and ugly

It will only last a little while

Stay here in my arms

I'll love you like Jacob loved Rachel

He worked hard for her

Run with you on my back

If you grow tired after all, we started this fire

This exceptional fire called love

I got ... you got it

We made it on earth

Life With Me

Vacate with me

Taste life past perception

I could never neglect you

Star chase with me

Past mars but still safe

I will always protect you

I shift gears when I speak

While this world stays on repeat

Your place is with me

Locked

Heights I never imagined

Bending time

What a pace I push

To land where humans can't reach

In who's world do I breach

The power of meditation

The fear of wrongful relations

Has to exist in every dimension

To be pure

Yikes

Who born of earth can take on that task?

From breath to breath

Make it last

Through snares and daggers

A world with fire underneath

Day after day to get in

You have to repeat

Lord Willing, My Love

Robert Dawson

In the future, the moon won't matter

Night will be over, and the sun

Won't shine

Souls will celebrate or burn

Depending on their earth deeds

I dream of you for this life

Travel by sea if need be

Whatever time allows

As long as we exchange vows

We can get through this together

I've seen earth at its worst

Smiled when it hurts

Kissed lips that weren't worth it

Times are changing

Love me while my heart beats

Hold me when I can feel

I plan to cross the ocean

To medicate without the pill

Healing in your hands

Believing in what's possible

What if the world ends?

Not even that would be an obstacle

Maybe we can reside on an island

Or somewhere more tropical

Away for man's anger, the rage

To cause the end of the world

We are gambling with eternity

Risk it all on uncertainty

What I'm chasing after is forever

I want to be with you

To start this chapter

Love and marriage

As we await the rapture

Match My Love

Don't push my buttons; I'm not too hard to please

I'm a dreamer and warrior

Setting my sights overseas

You are beautiful and sensitive

Do set my weary heart at ease

I've seen people with bad intentions

Pretending they won't leave

I could never do that to you

Fly with me. I'll show you Pluto and more

A unity worth having

You are all I'm asking for

Merlo

The Pluto summer

Life moves so fast here

Loneliness is bad for the heart

I've traveled at speeds unseen

The paradigm shift in my soul

She played the biggest part

I've cried in darkness

To the world, I'm full of light

Buried secrets in mind

Turned rage into art

I could never love like this again

She knows my grace and might

Kisses that cure my ailing chest

Dark wine when the suns down

Nothing is like here

Nothing worth being around

I love my earth girl

My Reality

The Pluto summer

I don't have all the answers

I'll be wrong a few times

However, I won't leave your side

There's nowhere the truth hides

I've tapped into worlds I can't walk in

Had dreams on repeat then revisited

I almost had to taste defeat

Kiss me. I'm amazed by what you have underneath

Your lips stick all over my surface

Circuits Ignited there's so much we have to see

This world is cold and ugly

However, I won't leave your side

People are reaching but can't stretch past their pride

Why keep playing if you're past your prime

Too drunk to face it

There's nowhere the truth hides

Searching in hopes for all the trouble it finds

Reckless spirits wreck havoc

Robert Dawson

The Bible says the meek shall inherit the earth

I live in the home of the brave. We're wild and free

We can make it rain from those clouds you see

They wanna track us and supervise with drones

Ohh, for a little bit of control

This world gets crazy

However, I won't leave your side

On a Hill

Robert Dawson

Days on earth last hours

Fires lit in the evening

We kiss while the night's sky is pink

Wildfires rage in the west

Artists pull strings and move crowds

I don't mind loving you out loud

Gift of love brings some of the blues

Regardless of the risk, I'm choosing you

Hoping for smooth songs in the morning

Hearts connected speak to me no auto corrected

One Hour Away From Mars

Robert Dawson

The nerve of a nigga

The spite in man's tongue

Underneath the wide smile

What records are ex sponged

Lies need assistance from the lips

Death doesn't need your approval

Patience can only wait a little while

I can still see the moon

The chill I can feel from the ship

The stench of fear in my mustache

Goosebumps on my arms

No safety from harm

Almost to mars

Permission to Fly

Love is made in the evening

While the moon is in plain sight

Merlo in the glass while the bud is still burning

I've been yearning for you

Like a cool breeze through the trees

You refresh me, and I'm lifted

Shifting gears beneath the night's sky

Fireflies roam the valley

You pull me in like earth's gravity

Now I'm grounded

Pounding all my beliefs in you

Odd lights move through the mountains

Side conversations held other dimensions

While I'm my heart ensures the right decision

Can I take you on this trip?

Perspective

Robert Dawson

I find myself smiling at random times

This world is burning trauma rages

Liars cook the books and bend corners

Married men tip the strippers

Single women just crave sex in fear of heartache

Rumors of war and genocide

There's no need to watch the news

I only have eyes for you

Seen Pluto in the summer and returned

Same earth, different day

We cradle to weak until it's a burden

Who on earth is far from perfect

Oh, the fear of self-reflection

So many times, we're second-guessing

I know now for a fact

You're all I need

Play in My Dreads

Robert Dawson

I surfed the web

First-class on planes

Plunged back to earth

To lock us in

Angels fall like natives

To mock our sin

This world is cold and ugly

Dressed in designer

I love you for real

Not just in my shaft

I love you in my head

You elevate my craft

Leaning on your love

Like Moses did his staff

In all my days be my better half

To stimulate one's mind

To be held and rocked

Purple Sky

Kiss me while I'm warm

Earth is wild, and liars whisper

Parties influence the bodies

Blunts pass, and shots are taken

We live in a world of hope

I hear songs on different frequencies

Watching the people as they move

Heading nowhere

Excited to move in a circle

Glamorous shots in the evening

Let's toast to us

We found love before the time ends

You were just I needed

At the right time

Red

Robert Dawson

My thoughts are positive

Love songs on repeat

As I rage through these streets

It's the feeling that I caught

That has me like this

I'm happy

Breath of fresh air

In any moment of despair

The gratitude that just sits

Seven Thirty-Four

Robert Dawson

Cast me not away this hour

I've lived a foolish and brash life

Flirting with danger but never settled

I've landed myself the perfect wife

I almost cost myself dearly

Who knows why I'm like this

Whatever it is you like it

Don't try to fight what's taking place

What was without form now has shape

Let's escape. I have so many ideas

My summer will be yours

On Pluto where it feels like L.A in July

I'll give you every day in this lifetime

Seventy-Two Seconds

Robert Dawson

We just blew by the moon

Laughter and horror

Flabbergasted by fear

This is crazy

You look lovely

So glad you aren't afraid of heights

To plan never seems just right

You are the only plan in sight

Fireworks in my head

Sending shockwaves through the dreads

We're almost there, love

Two Glasses Of Merlo And Sativa

This world is burning cast me out to sea

The fearful move from shore to shore

The excitement in the cosmos

Something is bound to change

In this cruel world ruled by the strange

We roam foreign skies, watching thunderstorms

Laughing because we're happy

Is anything ever this good

Nothing taste this good

In this Stratosphere

I fell in love and it worked

She landed safely in my lap

Held tightly I'm so secure where I'm at

I've sipped wine on the west coast

Climbed hills in the heat

Just to be close enough

To feel your vibrations

Like a song finely played in tune

The Pluto summer

What a buzz this has started

Cheers to the light and heavy hearted

One day we'll all find our truth

Yes I believe one day we'll all find our truth

In this summer or the next or shortly there after

Hold on to love and enjoy each chapter

www.ingramcontent.com/pod-product-compliance
Lightning Source LLC
Chambersburg PA
CBHW072017290426
44109CB00018B/2271